LAKE DISTRICT

Wit & Humour

BEATRIX BASSENTHWAITE

BRADWELL
BOOKS

Published by Bradwell Books
9 Orgreave Close Sheffield S13 9NP
Email: books@bradwellbooks.co.uk
Compiled by Beatrix Bassenthwaite

British Library Cataloguing in Publication Data: a catalogue record for this book is
available from the British Library.

1st Edition
ISBN: 9781910551219

Print: Gomer Press, Llandysul, Ceredigion SA44 4JL
Design by: Jenks Design
Illustrations: ©Tim O'Brien 2015

At a primary school in Kendal the teacher came up with a good problem for her maths class to solve.

"Suppose, there were a dozen sheep and six of them jumped over a fence," she said to the group of seven-year-olds, "How many would be left?"

Little Harry, a farmer's son, put his hand up. "Nowt," he answered. "None?" exclaimed his teacher. "Harry, I'm afraid you don't know your arithmetic."

"Really, Miss?" said Harry, cockily, "And you divn't know your sheep. When one goes, they all go!"

Two elderly ladies in Dalton-in-Furness had been friends for many decades. Over the years, they had shared all kinds of fun but of late their activities had been limited to meeting a few times a week to play cards. One day, they were playing pontoon when one looked at the other and said, "Now divn't have a razzie, pet. Ah know we've been friends for a long time but Ah just canna think of yer name. Ah've thought and thought, but Ah canna remember it. Please tell us what yer name is." Her friend got a bit cross and, for at least three minutes, she just stared and glared at her. Finally she said, "How soon do yer need te know?"

The magistrate at West Cumbria County Court spoke sharply to the defendant, "But if you saw the lady driving towards you, why didn't you give her half the road?"

"Ah was going te, yer Honour," replied the motorist, "…as soon as Ah could work oot which 'alf she wanted."

Two rival cricketers from Threlkeld and Windermere were having a chat.

"The local team wants me to play for them very badly," said the man from Threlkeld.

"Well," said his friend, "You're just the man for the job."

Simon was down on his luck so he thought he would try getting a few odd jobs by calling at the posh houses in Ecclerigg. After a few "no ways", a guy in one of the big houses thought he would give him a break and says, "The porch needs painting so I'll give you £50 to paint it for me."

"You're life-saver, mister," says Simon, "Arl dee it reet away!" Time passes until… "There yer go. Aas all done with t' painting." "Well, here's your £50," says the homeowner, handing over some crisp tenners.

"Thanks very much," says Simon, pocketing the money, "Oh and by the way, marra, it's a Ferrari, not a Porsche!"

It's well known that when poet William Wordsworth went to Ullswater in the Lake District with his sister in 1804, he had been in low spirits and was 'under the doctor'. In fact the first draft of his famous poem 'Daffodils' actually read:

"I wander'd lonely as a cloud,
That floats on high o'er vales and hills,
 I really could've cried out loud,
 Good job I took my happy pills."

A lad from Workington was bragging to his mate: "Me computer beat us at chess, but it were no match for us at kick boxing."

In the hamlet of Torver, a couple are bickering…

Wife: "I'm telling you, there's trouble with the car. It has water in the injectors."

Husband: "Water in the injectors? That's ridiculous."

Wife: "I tell you the car has water in the injectors."

Husband: "You don't even know what an injector is. I'll check it out. Where's the car?"

Wife: "In Coniston Water."

Just before the big race at Cartmel, the trainer was giving last minute instructions to the jockey and appeared to slip something into the horse's mouth just as a steward walked by. "What was that?" inquired the steward.

"Oh nowt," said the trainer, "just a polo."

He offered one to the steward and had one himself. After the suspicious steward had left the scene, the trainer continued with his instructions.

"Just keep on the rail. You're on a dead cert. The only thing that could possibly pass you down the home straight is either the steward or me."

Two hawks were sitting on their perch at Lakeland Bird of Prey Centre at Penrith.

"Look at that speed!" one hawk said to the other as a jet fighter plane roared over their heads on its way to RAF Spadeadam in Brampton.

"Hmph!" snorted the second hawk. "You would fly fast too if your tail was on fire!"

A Workington A.F.C. fan was watching his team play Carlisle United in a packed Borough Park stadium. There was only one empty seat – right next to him.

"Who does that seat belong to?" asked Dave from the row behind. "Ah got the ticket for me missus," replied the Reds fan. "But why isn't she here?"

"Aas afraid she died in a tragic accident."
"So you're keeping the seat vacant as a mark of respect," said Dave. "No," said the Reds fan, "Ah offered it to all of me friends."
"Then why didn't they take it?" asked a puzzled Dave.

"They've all gone to the funeral."

A man was waiting for his meal in a Chinese restaurant in Ambleside when a duck waddled up to him holding a red rose.

The duck says, "Your eyes sparkle like diamonds, my sweet love."

"Waiter," shouted the diner, "I asked for a-ROMATIC duck."

A man from Maryport said to his wife, "Get yer coat on, hinny. Ars off te club."

His wife said, "That's nice. Yer 'ave nae taken us oot for years." He said, "You're not coming with us...Ars turning t' heating off when Ah go oot."

A lawyer from Durham and a businessman from Carlisle ended up sitting next to each other on a long-haul flight.

The lawyer started thinking that he could have some fun at the man from Carlisle's expense and asked him if he'd like to play a fun game. The businessman was tired and just wanted to relax. He politely declined the offer and tried to sleep. The lawyer persisted, explaining, "I ask you a question, and if you don't know the answer, you pay me just £5; you ask me one, and if I don't know the answer, I will pay you £500."

This got the businessman a little more interested and he finally agreed to play the game.

The lawyer asked the first question, "What's the distance from the Earth to the moon?"

The man from Carlisle said nothing, but reached into his pocket, pulled out a five-pound note and handed it to the lawyer.

Now, it was his turn to ask a question. He asked the lawyer, "What goes up a hill with three legs, and comes down with four?"

The lawyer scratched his head. He looked the question up on his laptop and searched the web. He sent emails to his most well-read friends. He used the air-phone to call his colleagues in Durham, but he still came up with nothing. After over an hour of searching, he finally gave up.

He woke up the businessman and handed him £500. The man pocketed the cash smugly and dozed off again.

The lawyer was wild with curiosity and wanted to know the answer. He shook the businessman awake. "Well? What goes up a hill with three legs and comes down with four?" he demanded.

The businessman reached into his pocket, handed the lawyer £5 and went straight back to sleep.

An elderly couple from Keswick are sitting at the dining table in their semi-detached house talking about making preparations for writing their wills. Bill says to his missus, Edna, "Ah've been thinking, hinny, if Ah go first to meet me maker Ah divn't want yer to be on yewer own for too long. In fact, Ah think you could do worse than marry Colin in the Chemists or Dave with the fruit stall in the market.

They'd provide for yer and look after yer when Aas gone."

"That's very kind on yer to think about us like that, Bill," replied Edna, "But Ah've already made me own arrangements!"

A lad from Whitehaven, who had just started his first term at Durham University, asked a third year, "Can yer tell me where the library's at?"

The older student said disdainfully, "At the University of Durham we never end a sentence with a preposition."

The new boy tried again, "Can yer tell me where the library's at, you muppet?"

Insurance Assessor: "What gear were you in at the moment of the impact?"
Woman Driver: "Gucci sweats and Reeboks."

Two elderly ladies were enjoying a small sherry in their local in Ambleside.

One said to the other, "Was it love at first sight when you met your late husband?"

"No, I don't think so," came the reply, "I didn't know how much money he had when I first met him!"

LAKE DISTRICT Wit & Humour

A bloke from Barrow-in-Furness goes into an artist's studio and asks if the artist could paint a picture of him surrounded by beautiful, scantily clad women. The artist agrees but he is intrigued by this strange request. He asks his new client why he wants such a picture painted and the bloke says, "Well, if Ah die before me missus when she finds this painting she'll wonder which one Ah spent all me ackers on!"

The next day the bloke's wife goes into the artist's studio and asks him to paint her wearing a big diamond necklace and matching earrings.

"Of course, madam," says the artist, "but may I ask why?"

"Well," replies the woman, "if Ah die before me husband Ah want his new woman to be frantic searching for all me jewellery!"

Fred's wife has been missing for over a week. The police liaison officer warned him to prepare for the worst…so Fred went to the charity shop to get all her clothes back.

Q: What's the difference between a new husband and a new dog?

A: After a year, the dog is still excited to see you.

A policeman stops a drunk wandering the streets of Carlisle at four in the morning and says, "Can you explain why you are out at this hour, sir?"   The drunk replies, "If Ah was able to explain mesel', A would've been home with the missus ages ago."

At a cricket match in Lindal-in-Furness, a fast bowler sent one down and it just clipped the bail. As nobody yelled "Ow's att," the batsman picked up the bail and replaced it. He looked at the umpire and said, "Windy today, ain't it?"

"Aye," said the umpire, "Mind it divn't blow your cap off when you're walking back te pavilion."

A County Durham man is driving through the Lakes when he passes a farmer standing in the middle of a huge field. He pulls the car over and watches the farmer standing stock-still, doing absolutely nothing. Intrigued, the man walks over to the farmer and asks him, "Excuse me sir, but what are you doing?"

The farmer replies, "I'm trying to win a Nobel Prize."

"How?" Asks the puzzled County Durham man.

"Well," says the farmer, "I heard they give the prize to people who are outstanding in their field."

A well-known academic from the University of Durham was giving a lecture on the philosophy of language at the University of Cumbria in Carlisle. He came to a curious aspect of English grammar.

"You will note," said the somewhat stuffy scholar, "That in the English language, two negatives can mean a positive, but it is never the case that two positives can mean a negative."

To which someone at the back responded, "Yeah, yeah."

Q: What's a Maryport man's idea of a balanced diet?
A: A pint of brown in each hand.

A police officer was patrolling the lanes outside Milnthorpe one night, when he noticed a car swerving all over the road. Quickly, he turned on his lights and siren and pulled the driver over. "Sir, do you know you're all over the road? Please step out of the car."

When the man got out of the car, the policeman told him to walk in a straight line.

"Ah'd be happy te, offisher," said the drunk, "If yer can just get the line te stop moving about."

What do you get if you cross the Morpeth Town F.C. with an OXO cube?
A laughing stock.

A DEFRA Inspector goes to a small farm near Walby and knocks the door of the humble, tied cottage. A young boy opens the door and asks what business the man has on his parent's property.

"I've come to inspect the farm for compliance with EU regulations, my boy. Where's your father?"

"You canna speak to him, he's busy," says the surly child.

"I shall speak to him. He's had notice of my visit," the Inspector retorted firmly. "Well, he's feeding the pigs at the moment," says the boy, "But you'll be able to tell me Da easy enough – he's the one wearing a hat!"

One freezing cold December day, two blondes went for a walk in Grizedale Forest Park in search of the perfect Christmas tree. Finally, after five hours looking, one turns to the other and says crossly, "That's it, I've had enough. I'm chopping down the next fir tree we see, whether it's decorated or not!"

A reporter from the Westmorland Gazette was covering the local football league and went to see Sedbergh Wanderers versus Penrith Rangers. One of the Penrith players looked so old, he went over to him and said, "You know you might be the oldest man playing in the league. How do you do it at your age?"

The man replied, "Ah drink six pints o' broon iv'ry night, smoke two packets of fags a day, and eat loads of bacon batches."

"Wow, that is incredible!" said the reporter, "How old did you say you were?"

"Twenty-two," said the player proudly.

An Arnside couple, Enid and Sidney, are having matrimonial difficulties and seek the advice of a counsellor. The couple are shown into a room where the counsellor asks Enid what problems, in her opinion, she faces in her relationship with Sidney.

"Well," she starts, "he shows me no affection, I don't seem to be important to him anymore. We don't share the same interests and I don't think he loves me at all." Enid has tears in her eyes as the counsellor walks over to her, gives her a big hug and kisses her firmly on the lips.

Sidney looks on in passive disbelief. The counsellor turns to Sidney and says, "This is what Enid needs once a day for the next month. Can you see that she gets it?"

Sidney looks unsettled, "Well Ah can drop her off iv'ryday other than Wednesdays when Ah play snooker and Sundays when Ah go fishing!"

Did you hear about the idiot who tried to hijack a bus full of Japanese tourists near Scafell Pike? The police had no problem finding him – they had a thousand photographs of the bloke!

Over a candlelit dinner in Keswick Susan's boyfriend, a Northumbrian lad, proposed marriage to her. "I love the simple things in life," she said with a smile, "but I don't want one of them for my husband."

A man went to the doctor and said, "I've just been playing rugby for Creighton and I felt fine but I got back home and I found that when I touched my legs, my arms, my head, and belly, it really hurt."

After a thorough examination the doctor said, "You've broken your finger."

A policeman stops a man in a car in the middle of Barrow-in-Furness with a sheep in the front seat.

"Arreet, what are you doing with that sheep?" He asks. "You should take it to a zoo."

The following week, the same policeman sees the same man again with the sheep in the front seat of the car. Both of them are wearing sunglasses. The policeman pulls him over. "I thought you were going to take that sheep to the zoo?"

The man replies, "Ah did. We had such a good time we're gan te Sands this weekend!"

One night an old couple in Millom were lying in bed. The husband was falling asleep but the wife was in a romantic mood and wanted to talk.

She said, "You used to hold me hand when we were courting, man."

Wearily he reached across, held her hand for a second and tried to get back to sleep.

A few moments later she said, "Then you used to kiss us, man." Mildly irritated, he reached across, gave her a peck on the cheek and settled down to sleep.

Thirty seconds later she said, "Then you used to nibble me neck, man."

Angrily, he threw back the bedclothes and got out of bed.

"Where are you going?" she asked.

"To get me teeth!"

A housewife went to the greengrocer's in Keswick. She picked up a lettuce and examined it. "Why is it that these iceberg lettuces just seem to be getting smaller and smaller?" she asked the shop assistant,
"Global warming," he replied."

A police officer arrived at the scene of a major pile up on the A56.

The officer runs over to the front car and asks the driver, "Are you seriously hurt?"

The driver turns to the officer and says, "How the heck should I know? Do I look like a lawyer?"

A man walks into a bar in Workington with a roll of tarmac under his arm and says, "Pint please, and one for the road."

A young couple were pulling up at their honeymoon hotel in Grasmere. The shy bride felt very self-conscious about the fact that she was a newly-wed. She turned to her new husband and asked, "What can we do to hide the fact that we are on our honeymoon?"

The young man thought for a second then replied, "I know – you can carry the luggage!"

Q: Why was the Hardwick sheep arrested on the M6?
A: She did a ewe-turn

After seeing a documentary on how inner city youths can remove the wheels of cars in under four seconds with no specialist equipment, the team at Silverstone decided to fire their pit crew and hire four youths from Whitehaven. As most races are won or lost in the pit lane, McLaren thought their nimble young fingers would give the team an advantage. The first race came along and the car drove into the pits. The youths went to work swiftly but the McLaren team boss noticed a real problem. Not only had the youths replaced all four wheels within four seconds but in another 10 seconds they'd re-sprayed the car, changed the number and sold it to the Ferrari team.

A farmer was driving along a country road near the village of Troutbeck with a large load of fertiliser. A little boy, playing in front of his house, saw him and called out, "What do you have on your truck?"

"Fertiliser," the farmer replied.

"What are you going to do with it?" asked the little boy. "Put it on strawberries," answered the farmer.

"You ought to live here," the little boy advised him. "We put sugar and cream on ours."

Albert, an extremely wealthy 65 year-old, arrives at Kendal Golf Club with a beautiful 25-year-old blonde on his arm.

His buddies at the club are all aghast. They corner him and ask, "Albert, how did you get the trophy girlfriend?"

"Girlfriend!" exclaims, Albert, "She's me missus!"

His friends are shocked, but continue to ask, "So, how'd you persuade her to marry you?"

Albert replies, "I lied about my age."

His friends respond, "What do you mean? Did you tell her you were only 50?" Albert smiles and says, "No, I told her I was 81."

At a school in Whitehaven, the maths teacher poses a question to little Lee, "If I give £500 to your dad on 12% interest per annum, what will I get back after two years."

"Nowt," says Lee.

"I am afraid you know nothing about maths, Lee," says the teacher crossly.

"Aas afraid too, sir," replies Lee, "You divn't know nowt aboot me da."

At the Drunken Duck Inn in Ambleside, a newcomer asked an elderly local regular, "Have you lived here all your life?" The old man took a sip of his ale and, after a long pause, replied, "Ah divn't know yit."

A passenger in a taxi tapped the driver on the shoulder to ask him something.

The driver screamed, lost control of the cab, nearly hit a bus, drove up over the curb and stopped just inches from a large plate glass window.

For a few moments everything was silent in the cab, then the driver said, "Please, don't ever do that again. You scared the daylights out of me."

The passenger, who was also frightened, apologised and said he didn't realise that a tap on the shoulder could frighten him so much, to which the driver replied, "I'm sorry, it's really not your fault at all. Today is my first day driving a cab. I've been driving a hearse for the last twenty-five years."

A high-rise building was going up in Carlisle and three steel erectors sat on a girder having their lunch.

"Oh, no, not cheese and pickle again," said Jim, the first one, "If I get the same again tomorrow, I'll jump off the girder."

Harry opened his packet. "Oh, no, not a chicken salad with mayo and lettuce on granary," he said. "If I get the same again tomorrow, I'll jump off too."

Owen, the third man, opened his lunch. "Oh, no, not another potato sandwich," he said. "If I get the same again tomorrow, I'll follow you two off the girder."

The next day, Jim got cheese and pickle. Without delay, he jumped. Harry saw he had chicken salad with mayo and lettuce on granary, and with a wild cry, he leapt too. Then the third man, Owen, opened his lunchbox. "Oh, no," he said. "Potato sandwiches." And he too jumped.

The foreman, who had overheard their conversation, reported what had happened, and the funerals were held together.

"If only I'd known," sobbed Jim's wife.

"If only he'd said," wailed Harry's wife.

"I don't understand it at all," said Owen's wife. "He always got his own sandwiches ready."

A farmer from Hexham in Northumberland once visited a farmer based near Keswick in the Lake District. The visitor asked, "How big is yewer farm?" to which the Keswick farmer replied, "Can you see those trees o'er there? That's the boundary of me farmland".

"Is that all?" said the Northumberland farmer, "It takes me three days to drive to the boundary of ma farm."

The Keswick man looked at him and said, "Ah had a car like that once."

The nervous young batsman playing for the Netherfield Cricket Club was having a very bad day. In a quiet moment in the game, he muttered to the one of his team mates, "Well, I suppose you've seen worse players."

There was no response...so he said it again, "I said 'I guess you've seen worse players.'"

His team mate looked at him and answered, "I heard you the first time. I was just trying to think..."

Q: What do you call a ghost that likes curries?
A: A baltigiest

Did you hear about the last wish of the henpecked husband of a house-proud wife?

He asked to have his ashes scattered on the carpet.

An Egremont rugby union player went to his G.P. and said, "Doctor, doctor, every morning when I get up and look in the mirror – I feel like throwing up. What's wrong with me?"

The doctor replied, "I don't know, but your eyesight is perfect."

A couple from the Cockermouth had been courting for nearly twenty years. One day as they sat on a seat in the park, the woman plucked up the courage to ask, "Don't you think it's time we got married?"

Her sweetheart answered, "Aye, but who'd have us?"

A man goes to his G.P. in Askam-in-Furness and says, "Doc, I can't stop singing *The Green Green Grass of Home*."

The doctor says, "That sounds like Tom Jones syndrome."

"Is it common?" asks the man.

"It's not unusual," the doctor replies.

A pupil at a school in Frizington asked his teacher, "Are 'trousers' singular or plural?"

The teacher replied, "They're singular on top and plural on the bottom."

LAKE DISTRICT Wit & Humour

A man rushed into the Wigton and asked a nurse for a cure for hiccups. Grabbing a cup of water, the nurse quickly splashed it into the man's face.

"What did yer do that for?" screamed the man, wiping his face. "Well, you don't have the hiccups now, do you?" said the nurse. "Nae," replied the man. "But me missus out in the car does."

Did you hear about the fight in the chip shop last week? Six fish got battered!

There were two fish in a tank, one says, "You man the guns, I'll drive."

A woman from Barrow-in-Furness called Brenda was still not married at thirty-five and she was getting really tired of going to family weddings especially because her old Aunt Maud always came over and said, "You're next!"

It made Brenda so annoyed, she racked her brains to figure out how to get Aunt Maud to stop. Sadly, an old uncle died and there was a big family funeral. Brenda spotted Aunt Maud in the crematorium, walked over, pointed at the coffin and said, with a big smile, "You're next!"

When the manager of Berwick Rangers F.C. started to tell the team about tactics, half the players thought he was talking about a new kind of peppermint.

LAKE DISTRICT Wit & Humour

A young actor is very excited about appearing at the Theatre by the Lake in Keswick and can't wait to tell his father.

"Dad, guess what? I've just got my first part in a play. I play the role of a man who's been married for thirty years."

"Well, keep at it, son," replies his father, "Maybe one day you'll get a speaking part."

Many years ago, a miner fell down pit-shaft at Haig Colliery in Whitehaven. The deputy shouted, "Have you broken owt, lad?"

"Nae," called back the miner, "There's nowt to break down here, only a few rocks!"

A gang of robbers broke into the Carlisle Lawyers' Club by mistake. The old legal lions put up a fierce fight for their lives and their money. The gang was happy to escape in one piece. "It ain't so bad," one crook said. "At least we got fifty quid between us."

His boss screamed at him, "I warned you to stay clear of lawyers... we had £200 when we broke in!"

For a minute Morpeth Town were in with a chance – then the game started.

Many years ago there was a dispute between two villages, one in Cumbria and the other in Northumberland. One day the villagers heard the cry, "One man from Cumbria is stronger than one hundred Northumberland men."

The villagers in Northumberland were furious and immediately sent their hundred strongest men to engage with the enemy. They listened, horrified by the screams and shouts. After hours of fighting, all was quiet but none of the men returned.

Later on, the same voice shouted out, "Is that the best you can do?"

This fired up the people from Northumberland and they rallied round, getting a thousand men to do battle. After days of the most frightful blood-curdling sounds, one man emerged from the battlefield, barely able to speak, but with his last breath he managed to murmur, "It's a trap, there's two of them!"

Three blondes were walking in the National Park near the Penrith when they came upon a set of tracks. The first blonde said, "Those are deer tracks."

The second blonde said, "No, those are horse tracks."

The third blonde said, "You're both wrong, those are cattle tracks."

The Blondes were still arguing when the 11.20 to Carlisle hit them.

A new dentist set up a surgery in Barrow-in-Furness and quickly acquired a reputation for being a 'Painless' dentist. But soon a local chap disputed this.

"He's a fake!" he told his mates. "He's not painless at all. When he stuck his finger in my mouth I bit him – and he yelled like anyone else."

There's a man in Berwick-on-Tweed who claims to have invented a game that's a bit like cricket; what he doesn't realise is Northumberland County Cricket Club's been playing it for years.

Pete and Larry hadn't seen each other in many years. They were having a long chat, telling each other all about their lives. Finally Pete invited Larry to visit him in his new flat in Penrith. "I have a wife and three kids and I'd love to have you visit us."

"Great. Where do you live?"

"Here's the address. There's plenty of parking behind the flat. Park and come around to the front door, kick it open with your foot, go to the lift and press the button with your left elbow, then enter! When you reach the sixth floor, go down the hall until you see my name on the door. Then press the doorbell with your right elbow and I'll let you in."

"Great. But tell me...what is all this business of kicking the front door open, then pressing elevator buttons with my right, then my left elbow?"

Pete answered, "Surely you're not coming empty-handed?"

"I can't believe it," said the American tourist, looking at the grey skies over Windermere, "I've been here an entire week and it's done nothing but rain. When do you guys have summer here?"

"Well, that's hard to say," replied the local. "Last year, it was on a Wednesday."

A young couple from Aspatria were doing some shopping in Carlisle. Having purchased everything they needed, they returned to the car park to drive home.

"Where's the car?" said the wife. "Someone's stolen it!"

They went off to the local police station and reported the theft. Miserably, the couple walked back towards the bus station but as they passed the car park, there was their stolen car, back in the exact same spot! On the windshield, there was an envelope with a note inside which read:

Please accept my apologies for borrowing your car but my wife went into labour and I had to get her to the maternity hospital. I am now the proud father of a baby boy. Please accept the two tickets enclosed for a concert at the Sands Centre tonight as a mark of my gratitude. Thanks.

The young couple's faith in humanity was restored and they went off to the concert and had a wonderful time.

They arrive home to Aspatria late that night to find that they'd been burgled and the entire contents of their house had been taken. On the front door was a note, which read, "Sorry, but we have to put the bairn through university one day."

A driver pulls up by a traffic warden in the middle of Kendal. "If I park on these double yellow lines and pop over the road to post a letter will you give me a ticket?" asks the driver.

"Of course, I will," replies the warden.

"But these other cars are parked on double yellow lines," argues the driver looking around him.

"I know," replies the warden. "But they didn't ask me to give them a ticket."

Have you heard about the latest machine in the arcade in Carlisle?

You put ten pence in and ask it any question and it gives you a true answer.

One visitor from Northumberland tried it last week. He asked the machine "Where is my father?"

The machine replied: "Your father is fishing on the River Tweed." "Well," he thought, "That's daft for a start because my father is dead." Next he asked, "Where is my mother's husband?"

The reply came back, "Your mother's husband is buried in Alnwick, but your father is still fishing on the River Tweed."

"You're looking glum," the captain of Coniston C.C. remarked to one of his players.

"Yes, the doctor says I can't play cricket," said the downcast man. "Really?" replied the captain, "I didn't know he'd ever seen you play?"

Anne and Matt, a local couple, went to the Westmorland County Show and found a weighing scale that tells your fortune and weight.

"Hey, listen to this," said Matt, showing his wife a small white card. "It says I'm bright, energetic, and a great husband."
"Aye," Anna said, "And it has your weight wrong as well."

A man walks past a pet shop in Barrow-in-Furness. There is a sign in the window that says TALKING DOG FOR SALE.

The man doesn't believe it, but he is curious so he goes into the store. He sees a Lakeland Terrier, walks up to the dog and says, "Arreet, marra?"

The dog says, "Arreet, laddo? Hoo ista?"

The man says "Nora! Thoo can really talk!"

The dog says, "That's reet, marra"

The man says, "So what is it like being a talking dog?"

LAKE DISTRICT Wit & Humour

The dog says, "Well, Ah've lived a fine, full life. Ah rescued Avalanche victims in The Alps. Ah worked as a drug-sniffing dog for t' FBI, and now Ah read to people in an old folks home five days a week."

The man is absolutely amazed. He turns to the owner of the pet shop and says, "Why would you sell a dog like this???"

The pet shop owner says, "Because he's a damn liar! He never did ANY of those things."

Two Ambleside Cricket Club players are chatting in the bar after a match. "So did you have a hard time explaining last week's game to the missus?" says one.

Two men were walking on the edge of the National Park near Dalton-in-Furness when a large tiger that had escaped from South Lakes Safari Zoo walked out into the clearing no more than 50 feet in front of them. The first man dropped his backpack and dug out a pair of running shoes, then began to furiously attempt to lace them up as the tiger slowly approached them. The second man looked at him confused, and said, "What are you doing?

Running shoes aren't going to help.

You can't outrun that tiger."

"I don't need to," said the first man, "I just need to outrun you."

"I certainly did, "says the other," She found out I wasn't there!"

A man from Kirkby Stephen decided to become a monk so he went to the monastery and talked to the head monk. The head monk said, "You must take a vow of silence and can only say two words every three years."

The man agreed and after the first three years, the head monk came to him and said, "What are your two words?"

"Food cold!" the man replied.

Three more years went by and the head monk came to him and said, "What are your two words?"

"Robe dirty!" the man exclaimed.

Three more years went by and the head monk came to him and said, "What are your two words?"

"I quit!" said the man.

"Well," the head monk replied, "I'm not surprised. You've done nothing but complain ever since you got here!"

Two blokes are standing in the Whitehaven Job Centre, waiting for their turn at the counter.

The first bloke says to the second one, "Ah have te buy me missus summat nice for our wedding anniversary and the benefits cheque won't cover it."

The second bloke looks up from his paper and says, "What date?"

The first bloke thinks for a while and says, "15th September."

The second bloke considers his next question. "What year?"

Without taking a breath, the first bloke replies, "Iv'ry year for the last twenty-seven!"

In Appleby-in-Westmorland , two neighbours greet each other over the garden fence.

"Arreet, marra? Hoo ista?"

 "Poor old granda's feel down deed this morning," says the neighbour, "He was out in the garden pulling up cabbages and he went, just like that – we think it was his heart."

"What a shame," commiserates the man next door, "What're you ganna do now?"

"Open a tin of peas," says the neighbour.

A council trainee on a site in Workington was surveying land about to be dug up.

The gaffer says to him, "You go and get the metal detector and check for pipe work, lad, and I'll get the kettle on and mash some tea."

The gaffer gets the tea going while his trainee starts work. Half-hour later the gaffer puts his paper down, next to his mug of tea, to find out how work is progressing and he finds the lad sitting on a wall scratching his head.

"What's up with you?" The gaffer asks. "There's pipework all over the place. Look!"

The young worker sets off across the land, the bleeper sounding continuously as the detector passes in front of him. The gaffer watches him, laughing, then he says, "Are you divvy or what? You've got steel toe caps in your boots!"

Down the Nag's Head, a group of blokes sit around drinking when a mobile phone on the table rings. One of the men picks up the mobile and puts the speaker-phone on.

A woman's voice says, "How are you, darling? I hope you don't mind but I've just seen a diamond ring priced £2000 and wondered if I can buy it? I've got your credit card with me."

"Of course, hinny, go ahead," answers the man.

"While I'm on," purrs the lady, "I've noticed a top of the range car I'd like. It's only £65,000, could I order that as well?"

"Of course, poppet," replies the man.

His friends around the table look at each other in disbelief as the lady continues, "And I've just noticed a pretty little house on Windermere, my sweetheart. It's only £750,000 - could we have that as well please?"

"Of course, pet," answers the man, without so much as blinking.

The phone call is ended and the man smiles at the others and takes a long swill of beer. Then he looks around and shouts "Any o' youse know whose phone this is?"

Ten women out on a hen night in Whitehaven thought it would be sensible if one of them stayed more sober than the other nine and looked after the money to pay for their drinks. After deciding who would hold the money, they all put twenty pounds into the kitty to cover expenses. At closing time after a few wine spritzers, several vodka and cokes, and a Pina Colada each, they stood around deciding how to divvy up the leftover cash.

"How do we stand?" said Sharon.

"Stand?!" said Debbie. "That's the easy part! Aas wondering how Ah can walk. Ah've missed the last bus to Cleator Moor!"